The Gospel Truth

The Gospel Truth

Living for Real in an Unreal World

MITCH FINLEY

WIPF & STOCK · Eugene, Oregon

Wipf and Stock Publishers
199 W 8th Ave, Suite 3
Eugene, OR 97401

The Gospel Truth
Living for Real in an Unreal World
By Finley, Mitch
Copyright©1995 by Finley, Mitch
ISBN 13: 978-1-4982-3201-2
Publication date 6/2/2015
Previously published by Crossroads, 1995

All quotations from scripture are from
the New Revised Standard Version Bible, Copyright 1989,
Division of Christian Education of the National Council of
Churches of Christ in the United States of America.

This book is for my father- and mother-in-law,
Maury and Gerry Hickey,
the best in-laws anyone could hope for.
Thanks for the countless kindnesses
you have shared with us over the years.
You're the greatest.

We are so used to hearing what we want to hear
and remaining deaf to what
it would be well for us to hear
that it is hard to break the habit.
But if we keep our hearts and minds open
as well as our ears,
if we listen with patience and hope,
if we remember at all deeply and honestly,
then I think we come to recognize,
beyond all doubt, that,
however faintly we may hear [God],
he is indeed speaking to us, and that,
however little we may understand of it,
his word to each of us is both recoverable
and precious beyond telling.

−FREDERICK BUECHNER, *Now and Then*

Contents

PROLOGUE
A Particular Judgment: A Theological Fantasy — 10

INTRODUCTION
"Do Not Love the World or the Things in the World" (1 John 2:15) — 22

CHAPTER ONE
"Do Not Fear, Only Believe" (Mark 5:36) — 32

CHAPTER TWO
"You Cannot Serve God and Wealth" (Matt. 6:24b) — 42

CHAPTER THREE
"Go . . . into the Main Streets, and Invite Everyone You Find to the Wedding Banquet" (Matt. 22:9) — 52

CHAPTER FOUR
"This Is How You Are to Pray: Our Father . . ." (Matt. 6:9) — 64

CHAPTER FIVE
"The Kingdom of God Has Come Near" (Mark 1:15) — 74

CHAPTER SIX
"Unless You See Signs and Wonders You Will Not Believe" (John 4:48) — 86

PROLOGUE

A Particular Judgment:
A Theological Fantasy

Q. What is the judgment called which will be passed on each one of us immediately after death?

A. The judgment which will be passed on each one of us immediately after death is called the particular judgment. . . . The sentence of this judgment is final and will not be reversed.

— The Baltimore Catechism (1949)

AN EXCEPTIONALLY LARGE BLACK BIRD spread its wings, squawked, and flapped reluctantly away from an old stone fence at the highway's edge.

Squinting his eyes as they adjusted to daylight after the dim interior of the bus, Jacob Wharton stepped off and glanced around as the bus roared away in a dark cloud of diesel exhaust. It felt good to stand and to move his arms and legs. Jacob coughed and waved his hand in front of his face to clear the diesel fumes from his lungs. He massaged the back of his neck with one hand to relieve the stiffness.

Jacob hadn't the slightest idea where he was, and, for that matter, he had not a clue as to where he had come from. His short-term memory took in a grand sweep of about the last sixty seconds, since he had found himself leaving the bus. Oddly, Jacob felt neither anxious nor fearful, only curious. The day was sunny and warm, and the fields on both sides of the two-lane highway were full of wheat that was golden brown.

Had anyone been watching, what they would have noticed first was this: Jacob was wearing bright yellow shoes that nearly sparkled. Below his tan windbreaker and rumpled brown slacks, from the ankles down, he looked like a Florida real estate salesman. Otherwise, Jacob would never get a second glance. He was neither old nor young, not tall and not short, and his thinning, curly brown hair was neatly trimmed. He wore no hat, and he carried no luggage.

Jacob coughed again, and then inhaled a deep breath of clean country air. He closed his eyes and took pleasure from the smell of wild flowers, trees, and damp earth.

As Jacob began to walk down a narrow dirt road that led away from the highway, a gentle breeze came up and it felt to Jacob like a comfort. He removed his jacket and slung it over his shoulder as he walked.

In the distance, at the end of the road, under a stand of venerable locust trees, Jacob could see an old man down on his hands and knees, in faded bib overalls, hammering nails into the boards of a porch that was long and wide. The white two-story farm house to which the porch was attached looked well-kept and so much a part of the landscape that it could have been there forever.

The old man, with perspiration slipping down his cheeks into his short gray beard, looked up as Jacob approached. "Good to see you, Jacob Wharton!" he called. "Good to see you, indeed." He smiled broadly as he sat back on his heels and wiped his face with a blue bandanna.

How could this old man know his name? The question occurred to Jacob, but he was not bothered by it, did not even feel like asking it. "Thanks," he said as he approached the house.

Jacob climbed four new, yet-to-be-painted wooden steps to the porch and stepped carefully over a pile of shining nails. "Tell the truth," he said, "I'm not sure where I am. Could you...."

"Best you talk to the woman of the house," said the old man holding up his hammer to interrupt.

"Oh, okay. Sure." The wooden screen door rattled as Jacob knocked a polite three times.

"She's busy upstairs," the old man added as he began to drive another nail. "Go ahead and let yourself in."

Inside the old-fashioned house Jacob felt as if he had stepped into the warm and welcoming home his grandparents lived in when he was a boy. It had a soft, lived-in feel to it, as if its natural purpose was to comfort the weary.

Off to the left in the parlor, a roll of paper with

neat little long and short vertical holes punched in it turned slowly, and an old upright player piano began to play:

> *In the good old summertime,*
> *In the good old summertime,*
> *You'll be my tootsie-wootsie*
> *In the good old summertime.*

Jacob stood still and listened, remembering the words, smiling, slowly tapping his right foot in time to the music.

"Welcome, Jacob, welcome! You're a sight for sore eyes and then some."

Jacob glanced up, and on the stairs, hurrying down in a long blue-and-white gingham dress, was a woman delightful to look at. Jacob felt a deep, warm attraction for her on sight. The woman wore no makeup; she was not beautiful in the manner cultivated by women who try to imitate magazine cover girls. She could afford to lose five pounds, but her beauty was natural and radiant, perfectly un-self-conscious.

Jacob smiled. He thought briefly of the girl he fell in love with in high school.

The woman gathered Jacob into her arms, and in her warm embrace he felt like he had been lost and found, as if he had always been her beloved and always would.

"Here," she said stepping away from him, her hands on his shoulders, "let me take a look at you." She was slightly taller than Jacob, and her smile was full of undisguised affection. Framed by thick, shining auburn hair, her face glowed softly with a light of its own.

Jacob scratched his chin and grinned like a schoolboy.

"You look fine," said the woman, "really fine. Toss your jacket on a chair and come on upstairs."

As he followed the woman up the deeply carpeted staircase, Jacob wondered what was going on. He was mystified by the genuine joy his arrival had inspired.

"Make yourself comfortable, Jacob."

"Thank you," he said. But with a sudden cold flash of anxiety he began to wonder if he should break and run or ride this thing out to the end. Probably better to keep calm. After all, there would be no sense in making a fool of himself.

Off to the left in the large room they had entered, two soft old Morris chairs faced each other at an angle. On a dark little table between the chairs, in a slim white vase, was a single red rose bud just beginning to open. Jacob and the woman sat down.

The floor was light polished hardwood, and the walls were freshly painted white. Two big windows, raised open a few inches, made the room airy and bright. Thin white curtains lifted gently with the breeze, as in an Andrew Wyeth painting.

In the far corner sat a big, sturdy old four-poster bed with a billowing light blue canopy. A colorful patchwork quilt and fresh white sheets were turned down revealing hugely plump pillows.

A steaming hot meal was spread on a round oak table in the middle of the room. The smell of hot corn bread and baked ham was unmistakable. The white linen table cloth was immaculate.

"Mm-mm, that sure smells good," Jacob said, smiling. He crossed his legs so that the bright yellow shoe on his right foot bobbed forward a little, back a little, forward a little, back a little.

"Do you like your new shoes?" the woman asked. Her breasts, as she leaned slightly forward in her chair toward Jacob, were wonderful, heavenly, swelling warmly above the top of her modestly low-cut dress.

"Hm? What? Oh," Jacob replied. "Yes, I only noticed I had these shoes when I got off the bus out there. They make me feel different. Somehow they fit; they make me want to do a little dance."

Jacob stood up and walked, almost skipped, over

to the window and back. Then he sat down again. "They make me feel like a new man."

"They're really you, Jacob."

As he looked into the woman's deep brown eyes, Jacob thought his heart might burst with sweet, sweet love.

"How about something to eat?" she said. "I cooked it myself."

"Thank you," Jacob replied, "I *am* hungry. That ham and corn bread looks good."

Jacob and the woman sat at the table in plain wooden farmhouse chairs. "Some of everything?" she said, and she helped Jacob to huge portions of ham, corn bread, and hot buttered peas. From a blue porcelain pitcher she poured a tall glass of iced lemonade.

"Tell me how things are for you, Jacob." She sliced a square of hot cornbread in two and spread butter on both pieces. Then she began to eat, smiling at Jacob, politely dabbing with the tip of her little finger at the corners of her mouth.

Jacob's hand paused in mid-air, balancing a fork full of peas, as he looked into the woman's glowing face. He felt a desire so sweet and so good that his heart ached. Deep inside, Jacob wanted to tell this woman his life story and leave nothing out. At the same time, he felt fearful of saying anything at all.

"Oh, my life is ordinary," he said casually, intending to keep the conversation superficial. But his voice began to work as if his mind and will had been gently short-circuited. He spoke from his heart, giving a compact summary of his life, with the nonessentials trimmed away.

"I have believed far more than I should have and far less than was good for me. I broke a promise once, a big one. I've been afraid of so much, and most of the time, as it turned out, there was no need to be so. Sometimes I feel so lonely. I was married, but something happened. I still think about her. I have a son and a daughter, and I love them more right now than I ever loved them before. I work long hours — in an office. I don't enjoy life much, and I drink more than I should. But the thing is — and I've never thought about this before — I can never get enough of anything. Lately, whether I'm alone, or working, or with other people, I feel empty. It's like...."

Jacob tried to swallow away the lump in his throat. "Sorry, I didn't mean to go on like that. I don't know, I haven't got much of a story. I feel so melancholy. What a life." He took a deep breath to try to keep the tears back, shrugged his shoulders apologetically, and looked up from the plate of hot food he had been staring into as he talked.

"Jacob," the woman said quietly, as if telling him a

wonderful secret, "all shall be well. Have you forgotten my love for you? My love is deep, Jacob Wharton, my love."

She left her chair, walked around the table to where Jacob sat, and drew him up gently by his hands so that he stood facing her, looking into her eyes.

Jacob's lips parted in surprise, and salty tears rolled down to the corners of his mouth.

"I don't understand," he said. "I..."

"Remember, Jacob. Remember."

Then Jacob's forgetting began to fade, and dark memories, cold and terrifying, came slowly as out of a distant darkness. The screech of tires on asphalt, as he stepped off the curb in the sunshine. The second that his head swam dark with pain. Then nothing at all until he was getting off the gray bus.

"Wait. Where am I?" Jacob trembled, his open hands went to his face, which had gone pale, and his eyes were wide with fear. "What is this place? How did I get here?"

Now there were tears in the woman's eyes, too. She pressed Jacob's trembling right hand to her heart, and looked into his eyes. Her voice was soft and steady, full of gentle compassion. "Oh, Jacob, my love for you, and my desire for you, is endless, absolutely endless."

"Oh," Jacob said vacantly. But as the woman drew him into her embrace for the second time and stroked the back of his head, Jacob's fear slipped away. She held Jacob in her arms and comforted him, rocking gently from side to side.

"Here," the woman said softly. Then, as Jacob stood back a step, she reached behind her with both hands to unbutton the back of her dress. She slipped her arms out through the sleeves and let the top drop away; then she lifted Jacob's hands and placed them on her breasts. He was filled with a love for her that was at the same time passionate and pure.

"Oh my God," Jacob whispered.

"That's right," the woman said. "And I have wanted you since before the world began." Then she walked Jacob Wharton to the big, sturdy old four-poster bed with the billowing light blue canopy, where the patchwork quilt and fresh white sheets were turned down. . . .

INTRODUCTION

"Do Not Love the World or the Things in the World" (1 John 2:15)

— ✚ —

LISTEN... LISTEN. The story you just read, in the Prologue, is a story about God's world, the world to come that is already here and still on its way, "the kingdom of heaven." There are two worlds, you see — "world" meaning not the earth but this: *a realm of existence and a way of life*. One world, God's world, is green; it's a world of exuberant life and truth, love and peaceful delight, a world of justice, quiet joy, passionate love, ready forgiveness and courage. The green world is the world to come, and it's already here, all over the place... but not entirely.

The other world is dark gray. It's the world of the false god, Status Quo, a world where always, just below the surface, fear and anxiety rumble along like a lumbering locomotive; it's a humdrum world where justice is subject to utility, and superficial fun and empty laughter are as close as anyone gets to joy. The gray, unreal world is here, too, but it's on the way out, slowly but surely.

The gospel truth is about both of these worlds because the two worlds, though incompatible, frequently are in the same places. Often, the green world shines through the gray world, but the gray world sometimes seems to obscure the green world completely. The green world is all of creation as it was meant to be by its Creator. The gray world has power and control to the extent that we, God's human creation, take refuge in fear and anxiety instead of choosing to act in faith and trust.

God's joyous laughter fills the earth and the vast, endless, starry universe. This is the gospel truth. We, however, take ourselves too seriously and not seriously enough; or rather, we take the gray world too seriously and the green world we find it difficult to believe in except now and then, here and there. We are "saved," "liberated," "healed," "redeemed" when we believe in and choose the green world, the world to come that is already here, and recognize the gray world for the cosmic illusion that it is. This is the gospel truth.

We are frail creatures, and we find it terribly difficult to believe in the green world, the world called into being by the Creator. Most of us, much of the time, live as if the green world is but a fanciful fiction or a fairy tale. "Wouldn't it be nice?" We forget that fairy tales are true. Most of us, much of the time, live as if the gray world is the only world we can believe in. We use that grim phrase, "the real world," and when we use it we mean the gray world. But the green world is the real world, and nothing is more unreal, in the long run, than the gray world. This is the gospel truth.

Of course, in the short run the gray world has a passing reality of its own. We hurt one another, we suffer, and we die. Our inhumanity to one another sometimes takes on gargantuan proportions. Injustice, cruelty, everyday meanness of heart — most of us get our licks in. We look around at all the gray in our lives and take it for the ultimate, final, once-and-for-all reality. That's when we slip-slide away; that's when we go wrong.

In just about everyone's life, of course, there are moments, perhaps a day now and then, when we stand up and shout for all to hear, or whisper softly to ourselves alone, that the green world, the world to come that *is* already here and on its way, is, indeed, the ultimate reality, the *really* real world. At such times we do believe that life, love, peace, joyful laughter, justice, and passionate love are what it's all about. The day we accept ourselves as loved by another human being, and love her or him in return, is the day when the green world breaks through and we embrace it with all our heart. The day we choose to love that person when he or she no longer seems lovable is such a day, too. The moment we hold a newborn baby in our trembling hands may be such a moment. A day when we are alone in sacred solitude and everything falls into place may be such a day, or an hour when we are with friends in true unity of heart may be such an hour.

Yet these moments, these days, these hours pass, and we turn back to the gray world, the familiar, widely agreed-upon "real world," and we carry on with but a dim memory of our heart's encounter with the green world. All the same, our occasional "Yes" to the green world is what counts, and that is the gospel truth. The reluctant "Yes" we mutter to the gray world, day in, day out, is of small consequence as long as we don't completely forget the world to come that is on its way and already here, as long as we keep alive the memory of the day, the moment, the hour when, with all our heart, we said "Yes!" to the green world. This is the gospel truth.

Augustine, bishop of Hippo in northern Africa some fifteen centuries ago, got it just right, in a nutshell, and nobody has said it better since. Nobody. In his *Confessions,* the first book ever written in the first person, Augustine spoke to God. He said: "You have made us for yourself, and our heart is restless until it rests in you."

That is the gospel truth.

Nothing but the Divine Mystery we call God can satisfy the restlessness, the longing, the thirst and emptiness of the human heart. Still, we go on giving it the old college try, by golly, knocking our head against a wall. From God's point of view, it must be hilarious. We feel an endless emptiness, loneliness, and — here's the hilarious part — we try to fill it with everything from a new lawn mower to a six-pack of beer; everything from the inane distractions provided by television to an almost endless list of addictions; everything from barely concealed self-pity as a way of life to workaholism. We will do just about anything to avoid the emptiness in ourselves that only God can fill, and our inventiveness in this regard is sometimes world-class.

When we choose to live in the green world, we find the grace to let our heart rest in God alone. We discover that loving intimacy with God goes hand-in-hand with loving relationships with other people. We learn that much of the time love is no picnic in the park. As Dostoevski has the monk Zossima say in *The*

Brothers Karamazov, "Active love is a harsh and fearful thing compared to love in dreams. Love in dreams thirsts for immediate action, quickly performed, and with everyone watching.... Whereas active love is labor and perseverance."

We discover that love and trust go together. When we trust God's love we find ourselves able to trust people as well. We discover that in human relationships, as well as in prayerful solitude, we find loving intimacy with the God who alone can fill the emptiness at the core of our being. This is the gospel truth.

Listen. In New Testament terms, the green world is the "kingdom" or "reign" of God, and the gray world is "the world." Sad to say, we often find the gray world easier to believe in because it is more apparent than the green world. We can see the gray world, taste it, touch and hear it. We can examine it under a microscope or analyze it with a computer, so it *must* be real. So we think.

The more intimate we become with God, however — the more intimate we become with the Divine Mystery — and the more we give ourselves in loving service to other people, the more evident it becomes that the green world is the only world that is ultimately real, the only one worth living in, the only world where the human heart can find the rest it is meant to enjoy and the adventures it is meant to have. Countless people, like Jacob Wharton, don't discover this until they die, and so the gray world continues to grab much of our attention. This is the gospel truth.

The small book you hold in your hands offers some hints about living for real — in "green world" terms — in an unreal, or "gray," world. It's about living with honesty, authenticity, realism, courage, active love, and hope. Each chapter is an attempt to evoke, in part at least, the spirit and contemporary meaning of a single, bottomless saying of Jesus passed down for nearly two millennia in the Gospels. This book is about how, in small everyday ways, we might cultivate a place where the reign or kingdom of God — the green world — can grow even now, although its final and complete coming is in God's infinitely loving hands.

This book is about living an authentic Christian life in a world frequently unsympathetic to such a project. In other words, the topic at hand is spirituality, and spirituality is inseparable from lifestyle, the choices we make about how to live our everyday minutes and hours, including — get this — how we spend our time and how we spend our money.

This book takes for granted that religion should be in the service of spirituality. If my religion doesn't nourish my spirituality there is something wrong with my religion, or, more likely, there is something wrong with my understanding of my religion.

The language of this book is that of the cross and resurrection of Christ and our participation — in the loving intimacy called faith — in that paschal mystery. Along the way, it is the author's modest hope to spark some new life into a few ideas that are very, very old.

CHAPTER ONE

"Do Not Fear, Only Believe" (Mark 5:36)

LOUIS MOUNTBATTEN (1900–1979) was a near legendary British naval commander and the great-grandson of Queen Victoria. When he was five years old, Mountbatten was reluctant to go to bed alone in the dark. "It isn't the dark," he told his father in a confidential tone. There are wolves up there. His father smiled. "There are no wolves in this house," he said reassuringly. But this was of little consolation to young Louis. "I daresay there aren't," he replied, "but I *think* there are."

This is the way we live our lives, live our lives, live our lives, this is the way we live our lives in the unreal world: *thinking* there are wolves up there... or out there, or waiting just around the corner to devour us. We are afraid, and no matter what we do to protect ourselves we can't stop being afraid. No matter how much financial security we have, it isn't enough to stop being afraid of not having enough financial security.

Indeed, our national economy depends in large part on everyone being afraid. Think of all we are afraid of and of all the things we buy to try to make the fear go away. We buy insurance policies by the truckload, make financial investments, and "plan for the future." We worry about our retirement and talk about the need for common sense and practicality, but the truth is that behind all our talk we are motivated by pure cold fear. We are afraid that terrible things will befall us if we don't protect ourselves financially. Deep down inside we are terrified by the wolves we *think* are there, and because we *think* they are there we act as if they *are* there.

We buy everything from underarm deodorants to new clothes because we are afraid of something. We are afraid our natural body odor will offend other people, who will then dislike us. So as a society we spend billions of dollars a year on underarm deodorants and antiperspirants. This is a fear no one knew anything about before about 1950! Then we were "enlightened" by the advertising agencies hired to inform us about how bad we smelled and about the deodorants we could buy to remedy the problem. Lucky us.

We are afraid our clothes may not look quite right or are unfashionable, so we buy new ones so others will not think less of us. We are afraid of what other people will think if we drive a beat-up car, so we buy a new one. If we can't afford a new car, we feel bad about ourselves, and we *think* people think less of us as a result. The self-esteem of the average person depends greatly on the car he or she drives.

As a nation, we are afraid that other nations will harm us so we spend billions upon billions of dollars to stockpile weapons and maintain huge military organizations. The only way to maintain peace, we believe, is to make sure other countries are afraid of us, and there is an insidious truth at work here. Still, we spend vastly more to keep other countries afraid of us than we do on foreign aid and on programs such as the Peace Corps, the purpose of which is to make friends, not enemies. As a nation, we are afraid, so we make other nations afraid of us to protect ourselves. Fear builds upon fear.

In our society, fear is a way of life, from the ground up. We use fear of bad grades to motivate children and young people in school. We use fear of financial insecurity to keep people working at jobs they detest. Financial security is a carrot. We say, "Work at this job for thirty years, and we will give you a (small) pension after you retire."

Now the point is not that financial planning is bad. The point is not that retirement pensions are bad. Far from it. Employers owe it in justice to be concerned about such things. The point is that we waste so much of our spiritual and emotional energy on being afraid of wolves that are not there. Insurance company actuarial tables to the contrary, the odds are in our favor. The odds are that something terrible will not happen to a given individual. The odds are that the insurance company will make a huge profit from the insurance premiums people pay to make the wolves go away, and — wonder of wonders — that's exactly what happens.

A few years ago, a young man who was an acquaintance of my good spouse and me died suddenly. One day his wife and three young children had an apparently healthy, strong husband and father. The next day he was dead from a burst aneurism in his brain. Shocked by this, we decided to buy — you guessed it — an insurance policy. Within days we became the owners of mortgage insurance. That way, if either of us died suddenly the other one would have no more house payments to worry about. Fear motivated us to buy this insurance policy. We feared that what happened to our young acquaintance *might* happen to us, though the odds that this will happen are extremely small.

A mortgage insurance policy is not bad. It may be a perfectly prudent thing to buy. But to buy such an insurance policy out of fear is not a spiritually healthy action. If we would live for real in an unreal world, we would purchase mortgage insurance simply as a realistic precaution. Our heart would not be in it, you might say. The strange thing about insurance policies is this: when we buy them out of fear our fear does not go away; at best it slips into hiding. Before long, we begin to feel anxious again. Do we have *enough* insurance? Think of all the terrible things that can happen. Are we protected *enough?* Of course, there is no such thing as enough because no insurance company can protect us completely against all the wolves that *might* be out there. Besides, few people could afford to buy that much insurance.

Ultimately, of course, we die, and that is what we are afraid of. All fear, especially the fear of death, is a failure to believe, to trust in God's love. Yet the heart of Jesus' message is that God's love is absolutely reliable. That is the gospel, the good news. Jesus invites us to turn loose of fear, to stop worrying, and act as if the gospel is true. Our problem is that the good news sounds too good to be true, so we have a tough time believing it. Ah, me.

"Do not worry about anything," St. Paul says in the Letter to the Philippians, "but in everything by prayer and supplication with thanksgiving let your requests be made known to God. And the peace of God, which surpasses all understanding, will guard your hearts and your minds in Christ Jesus" (4:6–7).

When he wrote these words, of course, Paul only echoed the teaching of Jesus. In Matthew's Gospel, in particular in the Sermon on the Mount, Jesus lays great emphasis on the need to stop worrying. "Therefore I tell you, do not worry..." (6:25). "And why do you worry...?" (6:28). "Therefore do not worry..." (6:31). "So do not worry about tomorrow..." (6:34). "...do not worry..." (10:19).

The idea, of course, is not to be irresponsible. Now and then, some off-the-wall group of well-meaning but deluded people climb a mountain in California and wait for Jesus to come and take them away on a cloud. Now and then, someone reads certain New Testament passages and decides that God wants him or her to do nothing. The person quits working, sells everything, and waits for God to take care of everything. This is reading the scriptures apart from a basic source of divine revelation, a basic source of God's word even, which we all must consult daily. It's called Common Sense.

Over the mantel in the Hind's Head Hotel, in

England, you will find the following words: "Fear knocked at the door. Faith answered. No one was there."

This is how it goes: not to deny our feelings of fear, not to pretend we don't feel anxious, not to make believe that we're not worried about the future. When fear knocks, we need to go answer the door, but with faith in our heart. When we do this, we discover that no one is there, that our fear is unfounded, there are no wolves out there.

The most effective response to fear of anything, from fear of the opinions of others to fear of death itself, is...prayer, especially the kind of prayer that requires us to sit still, be quietly present to God, and keep our big mouth shut. For in such prayer we remember that we are never separated from our ultimate source of security. Though death is certain, though we stand before a firing squad, God's love is more certain. "For I am convinced," Paul declared, "that neither death, nor life, nor angels, nor rulers, nor things present, nor things to come, nor powers, nor height, nor depth, nor anything else in all creation, will be able to separate us from the love of God in Christ Jesus our Lord" (Rom. 8:38–39).

The First Letter of John trumpets one simple yet profound thought about the relationship between love and fear: "There is no fear in love, but perfect love casts out fear; for fear has to do with punishment, and whoever fears has not reached perfection in love" (4:18).

Love and fear are incompatible. If a person could love perfectly, he or she would feel no fear at all. When we are afraid, the main reason is our belief that God or other people are going to throttle us. But this just shows that we do not know how to love as we could. We are still afraid, and when fear knocks at the door we cower in the corner rather than open the door with faith in our heart.

The 1970 version of the New American Bible New Testament included a felicitous translation of the verse from Mark's Gospel at the beginning of this chapter. It goes like this: "Fear is useless. What is needed is trust."

CHAPTER TWO

"You Cannot Serve God and Wealth"
(Matt. 6:24b)

T**HE NATURALIST** and wilderness preservationist John Muir (1838–1914) cared little for money. But on one occasion he announced that he was wealthier than the millionaire industrialist E. H. Harriman. "I have all the money I want," Muir said, "and he hasn't."

That's the nub of the matter, of course. Most of us do not have all the money — and the things money can buy — that we want. We want more, and should we get more we want still more. We know the meaning of "enough," but we do not *experience* it for long. Once we get what we wanted, in a few hours or days we want something more. That's the way life is in the unreal world.

To live for real in an unreal world, we need to develop a spirituality of enough, a spirituality of limits, which is a spirituality of spiritual freedom. This spiritual freedom is both freedom *from* and freedom *to*. It is freedom *from* cultural pressures to be dissatisfied with what we have. It is freedom *to* be satisfied with what we have and give love of God and neighbor first place in our everyday life. This means, for example, keeping work and the rest of our life in a healthy balance. It means, for example, being a prayerful person, a thoughtful person, a person for whom spending time with family and friends is a major priority.

In Matthew's Sermon on the Mount, Jesus declares: "Blessed are the poor in spirit, for theirs is the kingdom of heaven" (Matt. 5:3). In other words, blessed are those who depend on God, for theirs is the green world, the real world. To live for real in an unreal world, we need to cultivate poverty of spirit. We need to cultivate an inner life that is free from dependence on anything but God for peace of mind and heart. The very idea of spiritual poverty is abhorrent in the unreal world. To deprive ourselves of anything within our grasp! How awful! On the contrary, Jesus says, willingly empty yourself so God may fill you with divine life.

There is a practical way to cultivate spiritual poverty and the freedom that comes with it. It is called fasting. There is a subtle but powerful connection between the temporary choice not to satisfy our hungers and growth in spiritual freedom. Some people prayerfully fast from solid food one day a week, for example. Others choose to prayerfully fast from television-watching on certain days and, perhaps, during all of Lent.

Most of the "reality" that television keeps people in touch with is unreality, the unreal world. This is so because television's perspective is skewed by an entertainment mentality. The television medium, in itself, has enormous potential for good, but as our culture uses it television is best taken in very small amounts. Nothing makes it onto television, even the news programs, unless it is entertaining. Quite often, the most significant human events get little if any attention from television because they have no entertainment value.

Take religion for example. According to polls, 90 percent of Americans say they believe in God or "a higher power." Eight out of ten say that prayer is a regular part of their life. Forty-eight percent attend religious services, and on any given weekend there are more people in houses of worship than attend major-league baseball games all year. Yet aside from the occasional visit by the pope, bizarre behavior by cults, or sensational news about pedophiliac priests, religion hardly ever makes an appearance on news shows.

The television networks claim to mirror all of life "out there." But according to the Media Research Center in Alexandria, Virginia, in 1993 evening news shows on ABC, NBC, CBS, CNN, and PBS broadcast only 212 religion stories out of more than 18,000 stories aired. Religion plays an important part in many public issues, education one of the most prominent, but to judge by what television news programs give us, religion is peripheral to life in our society, at best.

To limit our television-watching is to limit our exposure to a distorted, unreal perspective on life and the world and, thus, to live a bit more for real. To empty oneself by fasting from food or television is to make spiritual room or space for God to enter, and where God is there is freedom and reality.

As long as we constantly stuff ourselves on food, on the mindless and distorted distractions offered by television, on the endless river of "stuff" rampant consumerism offers, we will never be satisfied. But when we purposely empty ourselves, distance ourselves from such things, free ourselves from servitude to "stuff," then we cultivate the poverty of spirit we need to enter the "kingdom of God," the green world — even here, even now.

The thing is, most of the time the emptiness we

gain by fasting from food or television still feels like emptiness. But faith, loving intimacy with God, tells us that what we feel is not emptiness but the *Abba* (Loving Papa) Jesus taught us to pray to, the Divine Mystery who transcends our ability to feel. Christian mystics over the centuries all insist that feelings are unreliable guides when it comes to intimacy with God. The more we live with this holy emptiness the more we realize loving intimacy with God as the ongoing basis for daily life, and the more we live for real.

Some people believe it is possible to have it both ways, to be close to God and neighbor and be an enthusiastic participant in the consumer culture too. "What's wrong with having nice things?" they ask. There is nothing wrong with "nice things." The trouble is that many people are willing to give up the wrong things for the wrong reason. They are ready to sacrifice time with family and friends to earn the money they require so they can buy all those "nice things." They are ready to work sixty or seventy hours a week to have more and still more money, so they can have a bigger, nicer house filled with nice new furniture and a newer, nicer car — or three or four cars. Then they are surprised when their marriage goes sour and their children become hell on wheels.

There is nothing wrong with "having nice things,"

but there is a great deal wrong with making the kinds of choices people often make to accumulate "nice things." Living for real in an unreal world often means being satisfied with the house and furniture we already have, because if we buy a new house and new furniture we may need to work longer hours to pay for them, perhaps at jobs we don't like. In Matthew's Gospel, Jesus asks: "For what will it profit them if they gain the whole world but forfeit their life?" (Matt. 16:26a).

Mark Van Doren (1894–1972) was a poet and a widely respected professor of English literature at Columbia University in the 1930s, '40s, and '50s, and he was the college teacher and lifelong friend of Thomas Merton. In 1939, Van Doren's *Collected Poems* won the Pulitzer Prize. When Robert Frost died in 1963, *Time* magazine said that Mark Van Doren was Frost's natural heir as the preeminent American poet. Once a group of young men asked Van Doren what they should do with their lives. The professor gave a clear answer. "Whatever you want," he said, "just so long as you don't miss the main thing!" When the young men asked what that was, he said simply, "Your own lives."

So often, so very often, we think our life depends on something outside us, but this is only partially true. We need food, clothing, and shelter. But after that we need much less than we think we need. We think we need not less but more because we listen to the propaganda of the gray world, the unreal world, instead of listening to the whispering of the green world, the kingdom or reign of God. If we are to live for real in an unreal world, we must make a conscious effort to not miss the main thing, our own life.

On several occasions, I visited countries in Central America and in the Caribbean. There I saw the most astonishing material poverty in the most beautiful natural settings anyone could imagine. In Jamaica, I watched people "pick" on hundreds of acres of garbage dump. I watched as young men ran to be first to scratch through whatever a newly arrived garbage truck — under guard by soldiers with rifles — might dump. I watched children with no shoes play in the filthy water that collected near a standpipe in the garbage dump. I peeked into a shack made of cardboard and scrap metal and saw an old man lying there dying.

In Guatemala, high in the mountains outside the capital city, I stepped into tiny huts constructed of dried corn stalks lashed together, with long dried leaves for roofing. Inside, the air was thick with smoke from the fire burning on the dirt floor in the middle of the hut. I saw countless people with eye diseases caused by spending so much time in the smoky interiors of the huts. Medical personnel told me of rampant lung diseases caused by the smoke.

Yet in the eyes of so many ordinary people in Guatemala, Trinidad, Guyana, and Jamaica, I saw the light of faith unlike I have ever found it in our materially wealthy society. I ask myself, is spiritual depth incompatible with material wealth? After experiences like these one is tempted to think so. But no. There is no goodness in human misery, just as there is no goodness in a culture blinded to authentic spiritual values by the constant search for more money, more possessions, more distractions, and more comfort. The answer lies in a sincere attempt to strike a spiritually healthy balance.

Countless saints and holy people give witness to simplicity of life as the way to leave room for God. But none ever articulated the ideal with as much poetry and quiet joy as a man who belonged to no church and stood for no particular religious tradition. I mean Henry David Thoreau (1817–1862), and in particular *Walden,* a book he wrote that should be required reading before graduation from high school and again for graduation from college. After that, one should reread *Walden* at least once every five years.

Toward the end of his life, someone urged Thoreau to make his peace with God. "I did not know that we had ever quarreled," he replied. This is the spirit that permeates *Walden,* a spirit of quiet harmony with God and with God's creation. In particular, *Walden* is a great source of inspiration if one would strive for simplicity of life.

"Simplicity, simplicity, simplicity!" Thoreau wrote. "I say, let your affairs be as two or three, not a hundred or a thousand; instead of a million count half a dozen, and keep your accounts on your thumb nail. ... Why should we live with such hurry and waste of life?"

Why, indeed?

CHAPTER THREE

"Go . . . into the Main Streets, and Invite Everyone You Find to the Wedding Banquet" (Matt. 22:9)

ENGLISH ARTIST AND WRITER Caryll Houselander (1901–1954) was, on first encounter, an odd duck. She had the habit of covering her face with a white powder so her face was as white as a clown's. Topped by a mop of naturally red hair, Caryll made a strange sight. Yet after a few minutes in her company, people invariably found Caryll to be a warm, kind, and caring person, someone they could call a friend.

Caryll Houselander sculpted in wood and considered herself to be an artist first, yet she also wrote books, especially during World War II. One of her books, *The Reed of God,* is almost a modern spiritual classic, so expertly does it discuss the nature of authentic faith and give the lie to its opposite, spiritual phoniness.

As a writer, Caryll Houselander was serious and to-the-point. Yet in her personal life she was what we today might call a "party animal." She believed that faith and dreariness were incompatible. In 1954, when she was dying of cancer, she clung to life with a passion, for she had always loved life and embraced it with gusto. She said: "I honestly long to be told 'a hundred per cent cure' and to return to this life and celebrate it with gramophone records, giggling and gin."

In the gray, unreal world, life is a problem to be solved, a source of worry and anxiety. In the unreal world, in fact, people act as if life is a *business,* for crying out loud. In his early novel *Herzog,* Saul Bellow has Herzog, his main character, write a letter to the president of the United States. He writes: "Dear Mr. President, Internal Revenue regulations will turn us into a nation of bookkeepers. The life of every citizen is becoming a business. This, it seems to me, is one of the worst interpretations of the meaning of human life history has ever seen. Man's life is not a business."

✦

In the green world, in the reign of God on its way and present even now, people attend to practical financial concerns with a light touch, with a playful spirit, even. Those who let the kingdom of God into their world are able to keep financial concerns at arm's length, in their hands rather than in their heart. From an authentic faith perspective, after all, money is not an ultimate concern. Theologian Paul Tillich defined faith as "the state of being ultimately concerned," but the object of that ultimate concern is supposed to be God and neighbor, nothing else. If money becomes an ultimate concern, then we place our faith in a finite, limited reality, which means we engage in good old-fashioned idol worship — false gods, you know — a popular practice in the unreal world.

This goes on in the unreal world. Vast numbers of people, more than a few of whom think of themselves as Christians, live as if money is the only trustworthy source of security, and so money becomes an ultimate concern. "No one can serve two masters; for a slave will either hate the one and love the other, or be devoted to the one and despise the other. You cannot serve God and wealth," Jesus says in Matthew's Gospel (6:24). All the same, we long to be wealthy. We buy state lottery tickets by the millions each year, fantasizing against all reasonable odds about large numbers of dollars. In the process, some people become joyless. Even people of faith quietly mourn each month when their lottery ticket does not make them multi-millionaires. In the unreal world, people never have enough money; they are never satisfied with what they have, and so they have no peace. The desire for wealth, however, is not the only source of a grim outlook on life.

In the unreal world, religion is a great source of concern. Talk about grim! Many so-called religious people are among "the grim of the earth." There are grim religious conservatives and grim religious liberals, and they are grim because they take God with the utmost seriousness. The God who is the *Abba* (Loving Papa) of Jesus does not want to be taken seriously. He wants to be *loved*. As for religion, it is supposed to facilitate the nourishment of our spirituality. If we take religion too seriously we soon become unbearable to be around.

Sad to say, many extreme religious conservatives are particularly prone to being grim about religion. They cling to an earlier historical vision of their religion, for example, because it provides absolute answers, certain security — the ultimate insurance policy. Such people do not have a theological problem; they have an emotional problem. So great is their need for absolute certainty about God's will, so deeply do they need assurance that they know what God wants, that they identify God's will with the pronouncements of human religious authorities, thus engaging in a yet another form of idol worship — placing a limited, finite reality in the place of the one God. Religious conservatives forget the words of John Henry Newman (1801–1890): "Nay, one cause of corruption in religion is the refusal to follow the course of doctrine as it moves on, and an obstinacy in the notions of the past."

This is not to say that there is no place for human religious authorities. Quite the contrary. When official religious teachers speak, they do so out of a living sacred tradition, and their words should be received with honor and respect. Most of the time, they speak the truth. At the same time, such official teachers have their blind spots, too, and a bit of historical research clearly reveals the mistakes or silly pronouncements they made in the past. We should never fail to listen to official religious teachings with the intellect God gave us in gear and with our heart open to the Spirit of God. We should also always cultivate a sense of humor, particularly with regard to religion.

"It is the test of a good religion," said G. K. Chesterton, "whether you can make a joke of it." Precisely! A good religion is one that is not an end in itself but a *means* to something else, namely, the love of God and neighbor. If our religion gets in the way of our relationships with God and other people, instead of nourishing those relationships, then our religion is not serving its intended purpose. When we are able to make a joke about our religion, then we can be sure that our religion is not our god. That's the trouble, of course. Too many people worship their religion instead of God. When it comes to religion, there must be times to poke fun at it.

Any religious person should get a chuckle out of a joke told by one of the characters in Nancy Willard's delightful novel *Sister Water*. "What did the Buddhist say to the hot dog vendor?" asks one character. "I don't know," says the other. The first character responds, "Make me one with everything."

The Monty Python movie *The Life of Brian* pokes great good fun not at Jesus but at those who take the Christian religion too seriously. Anyone who cannot watch *The Life of Brian* and laugh heartily takes his or her Christianity too seriously. In one scene, actors portray people in the crowd listening to Jesus preach the Sermon on the Mount, but they are too far away to hear clearly what Jesus is saying. "What did he say?" a man asks. "Blessed are the cheese makers?"

H. L. Mencken (1880–1956), that old skeptic, got it right, too, with a definition of Puritanism that applies to grim religion of any kind: "The haunting fear that someone, somewhere, may be happy." Bull's eye! If our religion doesn't help us to have faith, hope, love, and joy, there is something wrong either with our religion or with our understanding of it. If your Christianity isn't a source of joy, peace, courage, and spiritual liberation, then I have no wish to know the Jesus you know.

Take a quick flip through the Gospels and count how many times Jesus appears at a banquet, dinner, or other social whoop-dee-do. Clearly, Jesus was a party-goer. He must have partied rather intensely, because there was enough evidence for his opponents to accuse him of being on a serious toot: "The Son of Man came eating and drinking, and they say, 'Look, a glutton and a drunkard'" (Matt. 11:19a).

One might think that Jesus' first public appearance would be at some solemn event. Not so in John's Gospel, at least. Jesus' first "sign," or miracle, takes place at a wedding party (2:1–11) where the wine flows freely and Jesus makes sure that it keeps on flowing. He might as well have said, "Party on! Dance the night away!"

Christianity is not a jolly trip to fantasyland, of course. We don't pretend there is no suffering, that there is no death. We don't pretend that life is a bowl of cherries and always walk on the sunny side of the street. On the contrary. We look suffering and death in the eye. We say, yes, there is a dark side to life, the world, and human existence. We see injustice and oppose it. We witness human misery and try to bring some relief. But at the end of the week, after we have done all that we can, we lay our burden down, and Saturday night we celebrate, sometimes quietly, sometimes with much noise, music, and carrying on. We party because we did all that we could this week, and in the long run it's all in God's hands, anyway, blessed be She.

There is an ancient Christian custom modern believers sometimes don't know about or, if they do, they overlook it. It's called Easter laughter. Karl-Josef Kuschel is a German theologian, and he writes like a German theologian. Sometimes you wish he would just *say* it, for Pete's sake, and spare us the verbal dithering around. Anyway, in *Laughter: A Theological Essay,* Kuschel explains that Christian joy "is anything but an optimism which suppresses problems. It is joy with a garland of mourning. It is joy with the cruel death of the cross behind it, joy which nurtures itself on nothing but the experience that the crucified Jesus did not remain in death but lives through God's action and remains alive in the Spirit.... Only in the light of this certainty can Christians, in faith in the resurrection of the crucified Jesus, laugh at death, that power which seems to be the strongest and bitterest on earth."

One thinks, too, of another remark Chesterton dropped. In his classic little book *Orthodoxy* he said:

"Angels can fly because they can take themselves lightly." We, too, are called by Christ to let the worry lines go from our furrowed brow and take ourselves lightly. Then, in spirit at least, we too will be able to fly. That's what faith should do for us, now and then, here and there, from time to time. At the end of the day, it is always time to let God do the worrying, at least until tomorrow morning.

In Jesus' story, the king instructs his slaves "to invite everyone you find to the wedding banquet" (Matt. 22:9). This image of a wedding party to which everyone is invited is meant to help us understand the reign or kingdom of God. A wedding party for everyone, that's how things will be at the final consummation of all things, when God will "be all in all" (1 Cor. 15:28).

Erk. *Everyone?* That includes people we don't particularly care for, everyone from the most respectable to the most disreputable. The rich and the poor, our friends and our enemies and the neighbor whose dog barks all night and keeps us awake, all are invited to the wedding banquet that is the kingdom of God. And what's more perplexing, since "the kingdom of God is among you" (Luke 17:21), if we are to let it happen in our experience we must strive, even now, to open our heart to all because all are invited to the wedding banquet.

People sometimes grow discouraged at what they perceive to be their own lack of faith, their inability to live the spirit of the gospel, or the fact that they can't seem to overcome personal faults or weaknesses. At such times, when peace and joy take flight, it can be helpful to recall the English novelist Evelyn Waugh (1903–1966). Waugh attended a dinner party in Paris, at the home of another British author, Nancy Mitford, where he was particularly rude to a young French intellectual. Mitford, angry at Waugh's social ineptitude, asked him how he could behave so meanly and yet consider himself a believing and practicing Catholic. "You have no idea," Waugh responded, "how much nastier I would be if I was not a Catholic. Without supernatural aid I would hardly be a human being."

CHAPTER FOUR

"This Is How
You Are to Pray:
Our Father..."
(Matt. 6:9)

IN ONE OF TELEVISION'S original *Star Trek* episodes, Captain James Kirk, Mr. Spock, and the rest of the crew of the starship *Enterprise* encounter a race of people who have lived on a distant planet for many centuries. Their most sacred words turn out to be a garbled version of twentieth-century America's Pledge of Allegiance to the flag. The words are scrambled to the point of unintelligibility, and the people no longer understand the meaning of the words. Still, the people's leaders recite the words as best they can because they sense that the words are sacred. Sometimes I wonder if we use the Our Father in a similar fashion.

The prayer Jesus taught his disciples is one of the most widely known prayers in the Western world. It is also one of the most widely misunderstood prayers in the Western world. Like any prayer that becomes familiar, we often don't listen to the words, and when we do listen we grasp but weakly the meaning of what we say. The reason for this is that we don't know what the words meant to Jesus and we don't know what they meant to the first people who prayed them.

There are three versions of the Lord's Prayer, or Our Father, one in the Gospel of Matthew (6:9–13), the other in the Gospel of Luke (11:2–4), and a third in a second-century nonscriptural Christian document called the "Teaching of the Twelve Apostles," or the Didache (Greek for "teaching"). The version in the Didache is nearly identical to Matthew's version, except it concludes with, "for yours is the power and the glory forever." Luke's version is shorter by a few verses.

Let us slog no further into the exegetical bog, however. If you want to know more about the differences and similarities between the three versions of the Our Father it's easy to compare them yourself. Instead, let us focus on the first two words of the prayer, from which it takes its name.

The prayer is addressed to "Our Father." Much fur flies today over whether calling God "Father" reinforces rigid patriarchalism in church liturgies, structures, and leadership. Some charge that if God is our "Father" then God is male, and that perpetuates female subservience and male dominance among Christians. Others reply that to call God "Father" is simply a metaphor, so there is no need to get upset. Besides, they say, we can't change what the Bible says, and to call God "Mother" is to engage in pagan goddess worship. Booga, booga, booga.

It is true that a metaphor is just a metaphor, and any metaphor has its limits. It is also true, however, that when we talk about and address the Divine Mystery, which transcends the human intellect, to say the least, all we have are metaphors. (In a Monty Python movie, *The Meaning of Life,* an actor dressed in bishop's miter and vestments stands in a Gothic cathedral and prays aloud: "O God, you are so very, very big!") When Jesus says that God is our Father, the point is that God is not a cold, forbidding deity, but a God who engenders life, nurtures, and guides us.

One problem today is that "Father" may not be the exact metaphor Jesus had in mind. The Greek word *patēr,* which Jesus uses in both Matthew and Luke, is a translation of the Aramaic term *Abba,* which is not best translated as "Father." In English, the word "Father" has become formal, somewhat stilted when used to address one's human father. Indeed, how many children call their father "Father"? Most children in our culture today call their fathers by a more familiar title such as "Dad," "Daddy," "Papa," "Pop," or "Pops." This is what *Abba* means; it doesn't mean "Father." If we wanted to pray the Lord's Prayer the way Jesus and the first Christians prayed it, we would begin, "Our Loving Papa," or something like that.

This means that when we pray, we address ourselves and open ourselves to a God who, metaphorically speaking, loves us like a big, gentle Papa-bear of a Papa loves his children, holding them when they hurt, rolling on the floor tickling them when it's play time, tucking them securely into bed at night, locking the door against danger. A Loving Papa is strong and gentle at the same time. That's the kind of God we have, Jesus says when he teaches us to pray, "Our Father."

Could we not just as easily pray to "Our Mother"? Of course. A pope, no less — John Paul I, whose papacy lasted only thirty-three days (August 26–September 28, 1978) — endeared himself to many when he remarked that God is our Father, but "God is even more a Mother to us." Again, we're dealing with metaphors here, so we should get what we can out of both the "Father" and "Mother" metaphors.

It is good to use feminine personal pronouns (she, her) to refer to God, and it is good to use masculine personal pronouns (he, him) to refer to the same God. Sometimes one, sometimes the other. Frequently today, writers and speakers avoid both rather than offend anyone who may object to either, but this may not be such a bright idea. When we avoid using personal pronouns for God, we lose a personal God, which leaves us with a cold, distant, impersonal deity, not the Loving Papa Jesus taught us about. Keep in mind, however, that while both metaphors — "Father" and "Mother" — are true, both are also false.

God is Loving Papa, God is Loving Mama, and God is neither, so don't take either too seriously, for neither has absolute value. The minute we take a metaphor too seriously we launch ourselves into yet another form of idol worship. If our faith is to be true we must love and worship only God, not the metaphors we use for God. If we allow our peace of mind and heart to be shattered when others call God "Father," we take a metaphor too seriously. If we allow our peace to depend on always using masculine metaphors and images for God, and never, ever feminine ones, we engage in metaphor worship.

I suspect that one of God's main messages to church people today goes something like this: "Thus says God: 'Lighten up, people!'" For those trying to be disciples of the risen Christ, prayer depends upon the cultivation of what an earlier generation called "detachment," that is, freedom from control by anything other than the Spirit of God. Thomas Merton put it this way, in *New Seeds of Contemplation* (1961): "We do not detach ourselves from things in order to attach ourselves to God, but rather we become detached *from ourselves* in order to see and use all things in and for God.... The obstacle is in 'self,' that is to say in the tenacious need to maintain our separate, external, egoistic will."

In Luke's Gospel, Jesus puts it plainly: "Those who try to make their life secure will lose it, but those who lose their life will keep it" (17:33). As long as we cling to what Merton calls our "self," our "external, egoistic will," prayer is almost impossible. As soon as we ask God to liberate us from what Merton, in other writings, called our "false self," then we can forget ourself and enter truly into the spirit of prayer.

So often, prayer ends up a self-centered litany: "gimme, gimme, gimme." Prayer of petition, asking our Loving Papa or Loving Mama for what we need, is perfectly legitimate. Never doubt that. But underlying even the prayer of petition should be the prayer of abandonment to the divine will. In the final analysis, our prayer must be the prayer of Jesus in Gethsemane: "My Father... your will be done" (Matt. 26:42).

It's not difficult to beg God for what we need, and it's not difficult to complain to God. Indeed, sometimes this is good and healthy. We might join Tevye, in *Fiddler on the Roof,* as he dances and sings his prayer to God: "Would it spoil some vast eternal plan if I were a wealthy man?" If we are angry with God, we need to give Her a piece of our mind. If we are thankful, we should tell Him that, too. We might call this the prayer of honesty, simply being up-front with God, telling Her how we feel and what we think, and asking Him our questions, maybe even demanding an answer or an explanation.

In the fifth month of her first pregnancy, a young woman suffered a miscarriage. Her husband did all he could to comfort her, but only after she raged at God, telling Him how angry she was at losing her baby, did she finally know peace of mind. "It was as if God said to me, 'I want this baby with me now,'" she recalled. "After that, I could let go and be at peace."

Many people find it difficult to pray at a regular time, on a daily basis, and there is nothing wrong with this. Many people pray off and on all day long, in the midst of their daily activities. Such prayer keeps us aware of God's loving presence in the most ordinary circumstances. Michael Leunig, an Australian author, wrote two utterly delightful little books (*A Common Prayer* and *The Prayer Tree*) filled with prayers that take their inspiration from the most everyday topics. In one prayer, Leunig rejoices before God in the wonder of — how ordinary! — hair:

We give thanks for the mystery of hair.
Too little here and too much there.
Censored and shaved, controlled and suppressed:
Unwelcome guest in soups and sandwiches.
Difficult growth always needing attention.
Gentle and comforting;
Complex and wild;
Reminding us softly
That we might be animals.
Growing and growing
'Til the day that we die.
And the day after as well
So they say! In all of its places
And in all of its ways
We give thanks for the blessing of hair.
Amen.

A prayerful spirit in the presence of a God who is sometimes Loving Papa, other times Loving Mama or Aroused Lover — as in the story in this book's Prologue — is necessary for those who would live for real in an unreal world. A prayerful spirit is necessary for those who prefer the green world — the kingdom of God — to the gray world, the world of ego, of self-centeredness, and of grim grasping for empty forms of security. Each of us needs prayer like a garden needs water, and the secret of regular prayer is that the more we pray the more we want to pray.

There are a gazillion books on prayer, and many of them are worth reading. Actually, however, prayer is simple. Too often, people turn prayer into a problem. Prayer isn't a nut we need to crack; it's a constantly happening process that, for our own spiritual, mental, and physical well-being, we need to be in tune with. The key to a prayerful heart is knowing that we need not do the praying; rather, to pray all we need do is attune ourselves to the Spirit of the risen Christ who prays to God, in us, at all times, when we are aware of it and when we are not. As St. Paul wrote, "God has sent the Spirit of his Son into our hearts, crying, 'Abba! Father!'" (Gal. 4:6). This makes prayer possible for everyone at all times.

CHAPTER FIVE

"The Kingdom of God Has Come Near" (Mark 1:15)

IF THERE IS ONE SCRIPTURAL CONCEPT that many people have but a vague understanding of, it's "the kingdom of God," sometimes translated "the reign of God." The original Greek New Testament term is *basileia tou theou,* and any translation fails to reveal the full meaning of the term intended by Jesus and by the inspired Gospel writers and editors. Still less does a translation into English communicate the implications of the kingdom of God for a spirituality and lifestyle.

"Kingdoms are clay," Antony declares in Shakespeare's *Antony and Cleopatra:* "our dungy earth alike / Feeds beast as man." Thus we see again how a metaphor — "kingdom" — has its limits when applied to a transcendent, divine reality. For the kingdom or reign of God is more unlike than like a human kingdom. Far from being mere "clay," the kingdom of God, like God's word, is "spirit and life" (John 6:63). This does not mean that God's reign is ethereal or otherworldly, that it has nothing to do with this world or this earth. Rather, the *basileia tou theou* has everything to do with this world, this earth, and this life. It is the ultimately real world, the green world all human hearts long for, and living for real in an unreal world means being open to, and preparing for, the reign of God at all times and in all circumstances.

An anonymous poet wrote:

His kingdom is coming; Oh, tell me the story!
   God's banner exalted shall be;
The earth shall be filled with His wonder and glory,
   As waters that cover the sea.

This is what the reign of God accomplishes, indeed, is already accomplishing: the total transformation of everything in creation as we know it. Magnificent as a perfectly clear, star-filled night sky may be, it is nothing compared to what the night sky will look like at the final coming of the kingdom of God. No matter how much joy and human fulfillment we may experience in this life, it is nothing compared to what we will know at the final coming of the reign of God. No matter how much pain and anguish we may suffer in this life, it is small potatoes compared to what we will feel at the final coming of God's kingdom, when "God will wipe away every tear from their eyes" (Rev. 7:17).

Many people think of the kingdom or reign of God as a religious concept in a "churchy" sense. Since the time of St. Augustine (354–430) theologians and official church teachings often identified the kingdom of God with the institutional church, but the New Testament makes no such identification, and recent official church teachings strictly qualify the idea as well. The Roman Catholic Church's Second Vatican Council, for example, in 1964 went only so far as to teach that the church "becomes on earth the initial budding forth of that kingdom" (*Dogmatic Constitution on the Church,* art. 5).

Keep in mind, however, that for Vatican II "the church" is first of all people, the people of God, not churchy institutions. So we, the people, become "on earth the initial budding forth" of the kingdom of God. "For, in fact," Jesus says in Luke's Gospel, "the kingdom of God is among you" (17:21).

In other words, the kingdom or reign of God is not an institutional reality but a human and universal one. It is the task of the church as the people of God to gradually "become...the initial budding forth" of the kingdom, and to serve, proclaim, and prepare for the kingdom of God, not to be identified with it. It is our task as God's people to do this as we experience the reign of God present "among" us.

Who do we live with, and who do we work with day in, day out? These people are not irrelevant to our spirituality and our gospel-based lifestyle. These people are, in fact, the ones among whom we discover and experience the kingdom of God. That motley crew you live with, those ne'er-do-wells you work with, they are God's people. "For here grows the body of a new human family, a body which even now is able to give some kind of foreshadowing of the new age" (*Dogmatic Constitution on the Church*, art. 39). Here grows the kingdom of God, here grows the real world, the green world, "among you."

Given our culture's artificial separation of the sacred and the secular, the holy and the profane, it is perfectly accurate to say that "the kingdom of God" is a secular concept, for in New Testament terms the reign of God is present everywhere, not just in explicitly religious situations. "If only we knew how to look at life as God sees it," wrote the French author Michel Quoist, "we should realize that nothing is secular in the world, but that everything contributes to the building of the kingdom of God."

Not to say, however, that we through our own efforts can "build" the kingdom of God. God help us if that were so, for if we have had some two thousand years to "build" the kingdom of God, and the world is still in such bad shape in so many ways, chances are we will never get the job done. On the contrary, the kingdom of God is in God's hands. Here and now, on this earth, the beginnings of the kingdom of God are already present in a mysterious but real way. At the final coming of Christ — whatever that mysterious notion may mean — it will be brought to final and complete fulfillment. Until then, Jesus says in Matthew's Gospel: "Keep awake...for you know neither the day nor the hour" (25:13).

At the same time, it is also true that human efforts are far from irrelevant. In the words of Anglican Archbishop Donald Coggan, "Wherever the bounds of beauty, truth and goodness are advanced there the Kingdom comes." When we work for peace among people, in our neighborhood, in our city, in our country, or in the world, "there the Kingdom comes." Artists and architects, bus drivers, publishers and labor negotiators, kindergarten teachers, medical professionals, church professionals, law enforcement officers, farmers, spiritual guides, and soup kitchen workers all advance "the bounds of beauty, truth, and goodness," and by doing so they open a place for the kingdom of God to slip into our midst.

Above all, we can see the kingdom of God in the person of Jesus the Christ, fully human and fully divine. In his earthly life he brought into human history the beginning manifestations of the reign of God, in his life, teaching, death, and resurrection ("resurrection" being a word that attempts to describe a real event we can't begin to understand or imagine). From him we can learn how to live for real in an unreal world. Earlier generations called this the "imitation of Christ."

The idea is not, of course, to knock ourselves out in a futile attempt to mimic the historical Jesus of Nazareth. The idea is to so open our heart to the Spirit of the risen Christ that our life becomes, however gradually, a unique manifestation of Christ's presence here and now. This is the core of any authentically Christian spirituality, and it has everything to do with every aspect of our life in this world, from our work to our sexuality, from our recreation to our mortgage payments, from our marriage and children to shopping for groceries and doing the laundry.

Sometimes people today think they can corral their spiritual life, organize it or "manage" it as they would, God forbid, a business or career. They rely on psychological tools like the Myers-Briggs personality type indicator or the enneagram to make sense of themselves and others. If I know what my Myers-

Briggs type is and what your type is, then I know right where we stand relative to each other and, even better, with regard to God. I can pin down my soul and your soul like a couple of butterflies on a specimen board. What a relief. Ditto with regard to the enneagram: it can be a way to avoid facing up to the complexity, unpredictability, and tough issues that commitment to a Christian way of life and spirituality can lead to. The enneagram and the Myers-Briggs can be — not to say they always are — ways to escape the mind-boggling mystery I am to myself and to others and the mysterious nature of my relationship with God. The temptation is to think that by using these things I can "figure everything out" and get it all under control.

There is something in the human heart that loves to latch onto a program. We like to grab a program by the throat until it yields up the answers and solutions to all of life's problems. I once met a husband and wife who were convinced that the world would be saved by square dancing! Some people cling to programs like Marriage Encounter as *the* answer, and to that end over and over they try to recreate the "high" they got from their Marriage Encounter weekend. Others give themselves heart and soul to the neo-pentecostal Charismatic Renewal as *the* answer. Still others do likewise with Cursillo.

All of these tools, programs, and movements have positive value, but we get ourselves into trouble when we fixate on any of them. Ditto with regard to a therapeutic or "I gotta fix myself" perspective on spirituality, into which an interest in the Myers-Briggs types and the enneagram can fit quite nicely. For some people, their spirituality becomes a lengthy search for their "inner child," while they conveniently forget that sometimes children are the most self-centered, obnoxious beings in the universe — almost as self-centered and obnoxious as parents sometimes are.

Others spend years as self-declared victims, trying to "heal" themselves of the harmful things their parents did to them when they were children. Again, there may be a need to rely on such tools, programs, or movements as "a stage on the way," but to fixate on any of them is spiritually infantile, at best. Do it if it seems helpful, experience it, but then leave it behind and get on with your life — that's the ideal for an adult spirituality.

The kingdom of God is "among you," Jesus says. He does not say that the kingdom of God is "in you" as an individual. If we are to make this the basis for our spirituality, for living for real in an unreal world, then our spirituality cannot be centered on the self, but only on God and other people. God dwells not in myself as an isolated individual but in my relationships with others, even when I spend time in prayerful solitude. This is the point of Jesus' often-repeated injunction to love God with your whole being and your neighbor as yourself. Jesus never said, "Come on over here, I got something to tell you: Love yourself." He always said, "Love your neighbor as yourself," and there's a whopping big difference between the two. If we forget about ourselves and love others, we will get all the love we need in return without grasping for it.

Obviously, we need times for prayerful solitude, or simple "alone time," to recharge our spiritual and emotional batteries. We need to make time to read a book or we won't have any new ideas to share with others. We need time for solitary prayer or we won't have the spiritual resources to share with others. But in these situations, too, the ultimate focus is on others. We make time for ourself for the sake of God and neighbor.

In the unreal world, people are centered on themselves. Sometimes they dream up ways to do this in the name of their "spiritual life," conveniently forgetting that Christian spirituality is essentially interpersonal and other-centered and requires forgetfulness of self, even death to self. In Matthew's Gospel, Jesus could not be more to the point: "For those who want to save their life will lose it, and those who lose their life for my sake will find it" (Matt. 16:25).

Bang. End of teaching.

In the unreal world, people dream up innovative ways to avoid the absolute mystery that is their life as it comes to them from God. In the unreal world, people use up a great deal of emotional and spiritual energy feeling sorry for themselves instead of feeling sorry for and helping others. All in the name of their spirituality, of course.

Finally, a truth of the real world, the kingdom or reign of God, that we would rather not hear. If we would live for real in an unreal world, we cannot sidestep the cross, pass it by, go right on to the resurrection. It just won't work, and our love will never be real as long as we try. In the unreal world, people try at all costs to avoid the inconvenience, pain, and suffering required by love. Those who try to live for real, however, take seriously the words of Paul and Barnabas to the disciples in Iconium and Antioch: "It is through many persecutions that we must enter the kingdom of God" (Acts 14:22).

There is no other way and, paradoxically, it is a way of deep and abiding joy.

CHAPTER SIX

"Unless You See
Signs and Wonders
You Will Not Believe"
(John 4:48)

── ✚ ──

YOU MAY CONCLUDE from the words of Jesus above, dear reader, that this chapter will focus on the need to give up childish wishes for miracles. You may think, "To live for real in an unreal world, we need to be realistic and stop hoping for signs and wonders." Typically, we read such words of Jesus and think that Jesus is shaking his head in exasperation. "You people, weak of faith, begging for signs and wonders before you will break down and believe. What a drag."

We may think to ourselves, "Well, it's true, I appreciate 'signs and wonders' as much as the next person. But I guess I should stop. I should not want to see miracles or put much stock in them.

My faith would be stronger if I would be more blasé when I hear about miraculous cures and that sort of thing."

But maybe this is not exactly what's going on here. Take a moment and read Jesus' words in the context they come from:

> Then [Jesus] came again to Cana in Galilee where he had changed the water into wine. Now there was a royal official whose son lay ill in Capernaum. When he heard that Jesus had come from Judea to Galilee, he went and begged him to come down and heal his son, for he was at the point of death. Then Jesus said to him, "Unless you see signs and wonders you will not believe." The official said to him, "Sir, come down before my little boy dies." Jesus said to him, "Go; your son will live." The man believed the word that Jesus spoke to him and started on his way. As he was going down, his slaves met him and told him that his child was alive. So he asked them the hour when he began to recover, and they said to him, "Yesterday at one in the afternoon the fever left him." The father realized that this was the hour when Jesus had said to him, "Your son will live." So he himself believed, along with his whole household. (John 4:46–53)

Observe what happens in this story. A "royal official," probably a Jewish functionary from Herod's court, approaches Jesus begging him to come and heal his son, who is on death's doorstep. Jesus' first response is, "Unless you see signs and wonders you will not believe." John says nothing about Jesus' tone of voice, gestures, or the meaning he intends by these words. All we have are his words. We automatically interpret these words in a negative way, as critical of the royal official's request for a miracle. But is it not possible that Jesus is simply making a statement of fact? "The fact is that you will not believe unless you see signs and wonders." Could this not be a simple acknowledgement of the way things are with us? Could this even be an acceptance by Jesus that this is the way we are put together? Is this necessarily a weakness or fault? Although obviously our faith cannot depend entirely on "signs and wonders," perhaps Jesus understands that the occasional miracle can be helpful, that we need something like this now and then, here and there.

Of course, like the royal official we must be open to the possibility of miracles before they are likely to happen. To live for real — to live according to the standards and values of the gospel — requires us to have a childlike, not to say childish, outlook on life and the world. We need to believe implicitly that even what St. Paul called "the cosmic powers of this present darkness" and "the spiritual forces of evil" (Eph. 6:12) are completely subject to Christ's power. In virtue of our childlike intimacy with God, our faith, we believe that the risen Christ is "far above all rule and authority and power and dominion, and above every name that is named, not only in this age but also in the age to come" (Eph. 1:21). One thing this means is that now and then, here and there... miracles happen, "signs and wonders."

Childlikeness is a basic characteristic of authentic Christian faith. Jesus says in Mark's Gospel, "Truly I tell you, whoever does not receive the kingdom of God as a little child will never enter it" (10:15).

At the same time, of course, in Matthew's Gospel Jesus counsels his disciples to "be wise as serpents and innocent as doves" (10:16). So being childlike does not mean being naive, acting foolishly, or expecting a miracle every time we turn around. Maybe what Jesus had in mind was something of a balancing act between openness and wonder at the gift of life and realistic cleverness. "Use the brains and common sense God gave you, but at the same time cultivate a childlike openness to miracles." That might be closer to the mark.

Now, there are "signs and wonders" and there are "signs and wonders." More than a few so-called miracles are phony baloney. Using our common sense and brains means, among other things, that we cultivate a large degree of skepticism when it comes to weeping statues, bleeding crucifixes, people who claim to have visions of and messages from heavenly personages, and so forth. We must ask ourselves, even "if" — and the if here is huge, indeed — such events are authentic, what do they add to what we already know from scripture and sacred tradition? Zip is what they add, that's what. You take authentic mystics such as St. Teresa of Avila in the sixteenth century or Thomas Merton in the twentieth century. Had anyone shown them a weeping statue they would hustle it into the nearest closet, lock the door, and say nothing to anyone about it. Had anyone introduced Teresa or Thomas to a person claiming to have visions and messages, they would avoid that person at all costs, especially if that person insisted on delivering divine messages.

What is a sign? What is a wonder? Surely there are times when miraculous or near-miraculous events take place, and such events continue to raise important questions for philosophers and scientists to puzzle over. Almost any physician will tell you that he or she has witnessed cures or recoveries that medical science cannot explain. Faith means being open to and accepting of such extraordinary phenomena.

Still, for most of us most of the time "signs and wonders" happen in a different sphere. They happen every day, and most of the time we overlook them or take them for granted. Living for real in an unreal world means we snap to attention, now and then, and see the signs and wonders that happen so often they become ordinary. In fact, our faith requires that we do this frequently.

Take the most ordinary of ordinary events, the fact that as you read these words your heart goes on beating — thump-thump, thump-thump, thump-thump. Pause for a moment and be aware of the rhythm of your heart as it quietly thuds in your chest. Now, how is it that your heart goes on beating? Do you yourself make it so? Of course not. Did you make it start beating in the first place, before you were born? No again. We may come up with a wonderfully precise scientific explanation for why a human heart goes on beating, beating, but does that really explain it, or does it simply describe what's happening?

Is it not a wonder of magnificent proportions that your heart continues to pump blood throughout your body? You don't keep it going by an act of will; it simply keeps on going, and that is a wonder. It is, when you stop to think about it, a miracle that cannot be explained. It simply happens. Well-known words from the Psalms, spoken to God, are the best we can do to account for this: "For it was you who formed my inward parts; you knit me together in my mother's womb. I praise you, for I am fearfully and wonderfully made. Wonderful are your works; that I know very well" (139:13–14).

When was the last time you took a moment to realize that you are "fearfully and wonderfully made"? That it is God who keeps your heart beating in your chest hour after hour, day after day? Talk about signs and wonders. This one qualifies any time, any place.

What about the miracle of friendship, the kind, for example, that lasts fifty or sixty years between a husband and wife? Where did this active, lasting love come from in the first place? Can we put it under a microscope or analyze it with a computer? No. Still it exists; it's real. Yet try to prove to anyone that it's there. All we can do is witness this love as it is lived out over the years. How does it stay alive? Wife and husband make the effort to keep their love alive, but ultimately it's a wonder, an everyday miracle stretched out over so many, many years. The wonder is not that there are so many divorces but that there are so many lasting marriages!

How often do we pause to wonder at such a miracle? Lord God in heaven, what hast thou wrought?

How can this be? That a man and a woman get on each other's nerves decade after decade, and make love decade after decade, and flail about through years of parenting, and still — oh, marvelous — stay married to each other. As young Motel, the tailor in *Fiddler on the Roof,* sings when he falls in love, "Wonder of wonders, miracle of miracles! God took a tailor by the hand, turned him around, and miracle of miracles, led him to the Promised Land."

How often do we stop to realize that over the years of a marriage God leads a husband and a wife into their own Promised Land? Is this not a sign? Is this not a wonder? Perhaps such common miracles happen to remind us of God's faithful love for us, but we don't notice nearly as often as we should. God knows we need to see signs and wonders, so She gives us signs and wonders every day of our lives, but we are too busy and distracted to see them.

Your heart goes on ka-whumping in your chest. ("I love you.") Countless married couples love one another year upon year upon year. ("I love you more than you can know.") The sun comes up each morning, and the moon waxes and wanes over a month of nights. ("I love you, I love you!")

Miracles are all around us, and we are too busy to notice. Notice, says God, and He opens our eyes each morning from sleep to a new day, a new beginning, another chance to see signs and wonders... if we will.

Blessed be God forever, who helps us keep on trying to live for real in an unreal world: in the already here, on-its-way, heavenly, earthly kingdom of God. Amen.